SRA

Reading Mastery

Signature Edition

Workbook

Siegfried Engelmann
Owen Engelmann
Karen Lou Seitz Davis

McGraw Hill **SRA**

Columbus, OH

SRAonline.com

 SRA

Send all inquiries to this address:
SRA/McGraw-Hill
8787 Orion Place
Columbus, OH 43240-4027

ISBN: 978-0-07-612464-0
MHID: 0-07-612464-9

15 16 17 18 GPC 19 18 17 16

Name _____

   •

• I am the best at doing magic.

   •

• I can hike up mountains better than everybody else.

   •

• I can read faster than anybody else.

   •

• I can throw better than anyone else.

Dan did not know how to ride a bike. He said, "I will try." Soon he was able to ride a bike.

Dan did not know how to fly. He said, "I will try to fly." Now Dan can fly a plane.

1. Dan did not know how to _____.

   • fly and ride   • eat and sleep   • run and jump

2. Dan was able to do things because he _____.

   • cried   • tried   • ate

3. What can Dan fly? _____

1. Where did the pack of rats live? _____

   • in a town   • in a hole   • on a farm

2. How many rats kept yelling and bragging? _____

3. Did the other rats like to listen to the bragging rats? _____

4. One rat said, "I swim so fast I don't get _____."

   • a cake   • wet   • sad

5. What did the rats slip into? _____

   • a hole   • a cave   • a pond

6. Were the bragging rats good swimmers? _____

Name _____

Fill in the blanks.

1. Tubby works near _____ .

   • Bay Hill   • Bay Town   • Bay Bee

2. Which boat was the fastest? _____

   • Tubby   • Wave Runner   • Red Cat

3. Where did the motorboats and Tubby stay at night?

   _____

   • Dock One   • Dock Two   • Dock Three

4. Which boat at Dock Three was dumpy? _____

5. Which boat at Dock Three was the strongest?

   _____

6. If a big ship ran into the dock, it would

   _____ .

   • smash everything   • stop   • fall apart

7. Which boat made a lot of smoke? _____

1. Circle the one who is sitting.

2. Box the one who is sleeping.

3. Make a **C** on the one who is clawing.

4. Make an **m** on the one who will get mad at the cat.

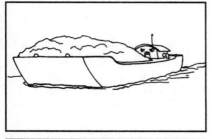

- I am the fastest boat in the bay.

- I push big ships and barges.

- I am fast, but not as fast as Red Cat.

- If I ran into a dock, I would smash everything.

- All the fun boats want to be near me.

- Fun boats say "phew" when they are near me.

Name _____

pig

9

1. Draw a roof on the house.

2. Circle the door.

3. Draw a pig under the word **pig.**

4. Box the thing that is a number.

---

hungry •   • one less than ten

angry •   • food you can pick from trees

nine •   • mad

pine •   • a tree that has cones

apple •   • not sleek

dumpy •   • when you want food

Lesson 3   **5**

Fill in the blanks.

1. What did Tubby do when she started to work?

   _____

   - honked her horn   - rang a bell   - flashed a light

2. How many times did Tubby honk her horn in the morning?

   _____

3. Tubby also honked her horn when she

   stopped _____ .

   - eating   - working   - playing

4. What time did Tubby start work? _____

   - three o'clock   - six o'clock   - noon

5. When did the motorboats leave the dock?

   _____

6. Did Tubby spend a lot of time watching them? _____

7. Some of the boats would ask Tubby if she

   wanted to _____ .

   - sleep   - sink   - race

8. At the end of the day, the motorboats got mad at Tubby for

   _____ .

   - sleeping   - making waves   - smoking

Name _____

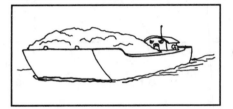

- Honk, honk, honk.

- I wish the wizard was here.

- **The wind is blowing one toward Dock Three.**

- I will try to scare the monster.

- This is not home. This is Rome.

- I push big boats around the bay.

- Away, away.

1. Write the word **shouting** in the box.

2. Make a line over the first letter.

3. Make a dot under the last letter.

4. Make a box around the letter that is before **u.**

5. Write the word **no** below the big box.

Lesson 4

1. At night, what came into the bay?

   _____

   • a fish   • a storm   • a tug boat

2. What did the storm push out of place? _____

   • a ship   • a boat   • a barge

3. The barge was headed for _____ .

   • Dock Three   • a ship   • the beach

4. Did the storm wake up the motorboats? _____

5. Did the storm wake up Tubby? _____

6. What did the barge do when it was very close to the dock?

   _____

   • honked two times   • flashed its lights
              • honked three times

7. Did that wake Tubby? _____

8. Who yelled, "Help us"? _____

Name _____

1. What was going to smash the boats at Dock Three?

_____

       • a wave   • a ship   • a barge

2. Who went between the barge and the dock?

_____

3. Did Tubby stop that barge? _____

4. Where did Tubby push the barge?

_____

  • into the bay   • into the dock   • on the beach

5. Why did Tubby stop out there?

_____

      • Her motor had blown.   • It was dark.
              • She wanted to play.

6. Who towed Tubby back to the dock? _____

7. Are all the boats pals now? _____

store •   • big

large •   • a place where you buy things

fast •   • not slow

tug •   • not awake

asleep •   • a boat that pushes other boats

 •   • It goes on your hand.

 •   • It likes to sit.

                                    • It almost rammed into
                                      Dock Three.

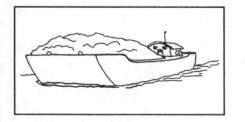 •   • It has new red paint.

Name _____

1. Rolla was unhappy because she was close to

   _____ .

   - a painting   • horse 8   • horse 2

2. What did Rolla do to get far from horse 8?

   _____

   - jumped up   • went faster   • went slower

3. When Rolla slowed down, what did the other horses do?

   _____

4. What did the music do? _____

5. Some of the other horses _____ .

   - went faster   • laughed at Rolla   • painted Rolla

6. When Rolla woke up the next morning, she saw

   _____ .

   - horse 8   • the moon and sun
   - mountains and valleys

7. Is Rolla happy now? _____

- I am king of all the animals.

- I am so strong I can move big ships.

- I can't take the vow of a genie.

- I want to find out more rules so I can get out of here.

- I changed a frog into a king.

| love | angry | skates | light | school | picnic |

_____   _____   _____

_____   _____   _____

Name _____

1. Make a line under each thing that Molly made.

   - phone   - robot   - toaster   - truck

   - racing boat   - pen   - folding chair

2. Did Molly make any things that were perfect? _____

3. What did Molly's toaster do to some of the slices?

   _____

   - burned them   - smashed them   - folded them

4. What was the best thing that Molly made?

   _____

   - a racing boat   - Bleep   - a folding chair

5. How many years did it take Molly to make Bleep?

   _____

6. Who did Bleep sound like? _____

7. Did Bleep always tell the truth? _____

Lesson 7   **13**

The boy walked home.

1. Make a line under the first two words.

2. Who walked home? _____

3. Box the words that tell who walked home.

4. Where did the boy walk? _____

5. Circle the word that tells where the boy walked.

lake	red	8	sheep	perfect

1. Help, a big wolf is after the _____ .

2. I slowed down to get away from horse _____ .

3. Red Cat and I both have coats of paint that are _____ .

4. The rule says that every dusty path leads to the _____ .

5. I am a very smart woman, but none of the things I make

   are _____ .

Rolla Slows Down

One day, Rolla said to herself, "I am number 1, but I am right behind number 8." Rolla thought that she should be far away from number 8. Then it would look as if she was the leader and the other horses were following her.

Rolla said, "I will get far from horse 8." To do that, Rolla slowed down. She went slower and slower. But when she went slower, all the other horses went slower. The music slowed down. The mothers were unhappy. One of them said, "This merry-go-round is so slow, you can't tell if it's going or if it has stopped."

The other horses were not happy with Rolla. Horse 2 kept shouting at Rolla, "Come on, Rolla. Let's get this merry-go-round moving." But Rolla tried as hard as she could to slow down.

At the end of the day, horse 8 was still there, right in front of her. That evening, horse 3 asked, "What are you trying to do?" When Rolla told them, some of the horses started to laugh. Then horse 5 said, "Rolla, would you be happy if you could not see horse 8?"

"Yes," Rolla said. "If I could not see that horse, I would not feel like I was following it. I feel like the leader." So the other horses did a lot of talking. When they were done, they smiled and told Rolla they would fix things up.

The next day when Rolla woke up, she looked in front of her and saw mountains and valleys. They were lovely. She couldn't see another horse anywhere in front of her. After a while, she found out that the other horses had made a painting and put it between her and horse 8. But Rolla didn't care. She felt wonderful leading all the horses into the mountains.

So everything is fine now. The horses are happy. The music sounds good. And the mothers and children like the merry-go-round even more than before.

The end.

Mastery Test 1

Name _____

Tubby and the other boats at Dock Three were sleeping when a very bad storm raced into the bay. The winds lashed out and rolled the water into large waves. Soon those waves were crashing against the docks. They were also crashing against the ships and barges. A barge longer than three blocks was blown out of place. That barge was coming right at Dock Three.

1. boy

2. p<u>o</u>int

3. slept

4. charge

5. thought

1. valley

2. stronger

3. robot

4. motor

5. course

1. became

2. pulled

3. heavy

4. against

5. mountain

Name _____

peach •   • It goes on your head.

hat •   • They fit on your feet.

glasses •   • You put it over a shirt.

socks •   • It grows on a tree.

coat •   • They help you to see.

   • I would love to eat a frog.

   • I'm much slower, but I'm stronger.

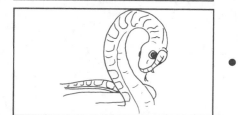   • Okay, baby.

   • But what and when . . .

   • I hate to see horse 8 in front.

Lesson 8   **19**

1. Who called Molly on the phone?

   _____

   • Bleep   • Mrs. Anderson   • Rolla

2. What did Molly and Mrs. Anderson plan to do today?

   _____

   • make a racing sled   • go swimming   • have lunch

3. Molly didn't talk to Mrs. Anderson on the phone because

   she was _____ .

   • in her shop   • out of town   • singing

4. Who talked to Mrs. Anderson on the phone? _____

5. Did Mrs. Anderson know who she was talking to? _____

6. Where did Bleep say they should eat?

   _____

   • at the lake   • at Fifth and Oak   • at First and Elm

7. What did Bleep tell Molly to bring with her?

   _____

   • a book   • a folding chair   • a racing sled

Name _____

- "Ott and I can train the new genies."

- "I can't take the vow of a genie."

- "Bleep. I never lie."

- "I think Bleep lied to both of us."

- "There is a good place to eat at First and Elm."

- "There is no place to eat at First and Elm."

Are we having fun?

1. Circle the first word.

2. Make a line over the last word.

3. Make three dots under the word after **we**.

4. Box the word **we**.

Lesson 9   **21**

1. What did Bleep load into Molly's van?

   _____

   • a cake maker   • a folding chair   • a folding bed

2. Molly drove the van to the corner of

   _____ .

   • First and Elm   • Third and Elm   • First and Oak

3. She parked in front of a _____ .

   • place to eat   • junk yard   • house

4. She parked in a _____ .

   • no parking zone   • pick up zone   • drop off zone

5. Who parked next to the red van?

   _____

   • Mrs. Anderson   • Bob   • Molly

6. Did Mrs. Anderson find Molly? _____

7. Who said, "I think Bleep lied to both of us"?

   _____

Name _____

1. Was Molly right in front of the junk yard when
   Mrs. Anderson found her? _____

2. When they got back to the corner of First and Elm, what
   was missing? _____
   - the car and the van   • the racing sled   • the cake makers

3. What do the workers do with anything left in the drop off
   zone? _____

4. The worker led Molly and Mrs. Anderson to a great big

   _____ .

   - pile of dirt   • pile of parts   • part of a pile

5. Why didn't the workers put the cars back together?

   _____

   - They didn't know how.   • They were tired.
          • They didn't want to.

6. Molly said, "We can get these cars back together by

   _____ ."

   - noon   • bed time   • dinner time

hat •   • something you sit on

book •   • something you eat

chair •   • something you spend

cash •   • something you put on your head

egg •   • something you read

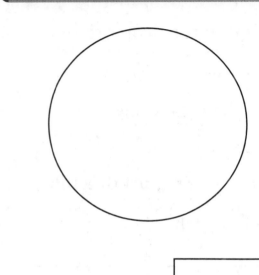

1. Write your first name in the box.

2. Write the word **cat** in the circle.

3. Make a box around the circle.

4. Make a circle in the star.

Name _____

1. Who worked with Molly and Mrs. Anderson at the junk

   yard? _____

   • Bleep   • four workers   • Bob

2. Who cried? _____

3. When Molly got home, she thought the car looked

   _____ .

   • red   • sort of pretty   • ugly

4. Molly thought about leaving Bleep at

   _____ .

   • a farm   • a no parking zone   • the drop off zone

5. Molly told Bleep that he could not

   _____ .

   • say "Bleep" any more   • talk on the phone   • drive a van

6. Who helped put the cars back together the right way?

   _____

   • workers from the junk yard   • workers from a car shop

   • Bob

- The fly was next to the cup.

- Something was on the side of a cup.

- The cup was on top of a ball.

- A bird was in the cup.

smile	clocks	mouse	smoke	school

mitten

Name _____

1. Patty was a mouse that was very _____ .

   • old   • small   • large

2. She had _____ brothers.

3. She had _____ sisters.

4. Who else lived with her? _____

5. Patty's voice was very _____ .

   • soft   • loud   • tiny

6. What other kind of animal lived in the house with the mice?

   _____

7. Her brothers gave her the name Big Mouse the Big

   _____ .

   • Month   • House   • Mouth

_____

1. Write the word **dressing** in the box.

2. Make a line over the **n.**

3. Circle the two letters that come just before **i.**

4. Make a box around the first letter.

5. Make a line below the last three letters.

shop •   • a little store

stones •   • Bikes have two of them.

wheels •   • It's cold and white.

trees •   • They have leaves.

snow •   • small rocks

| bridge | window | mouse | loud | ice |

_____   _____   _____

Name _____

1. One time, Patty shouted when her brothers and sisters

   _____ .

   - hid from her   - tickled her   - talked to her

2. How long was it before her brothers could hear well?

   _____

   - six years   - four days   - six days

3. That night, Patty's _____ gave her
   bad news.

   - mother   - brothers   - sisters

4. Who had to stay home? _____

5. Patty's mom and dad smelled _____ .

   - new cheese   - new mice   - new cats

6. Who was visiting Arnold? _____

   - Bob   - four cats   - four mice

Lesson 13   **29**

1. Write the word **somebody** in the box.

2. Circle the first letter.

3. Make a line under the word **some.**

4. Make a line over the last two letters in the box.

5. Make a box around the letter that comes after **d.**

friend •   • shout

party •   • They have feathers.

bedroom •   • a place in a house where you sleep

night •   • You eat, drink, and play games.

yell •   • The sun is not out.

birds •   • a pal

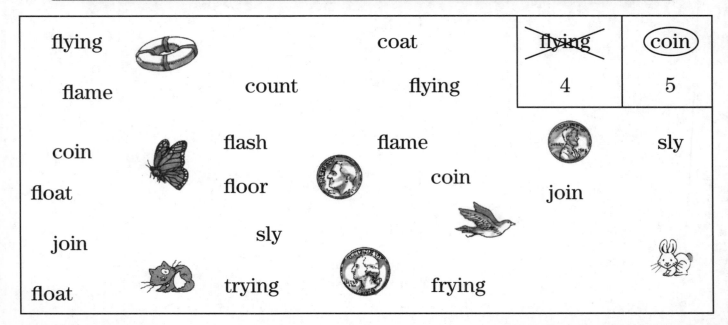

~~flying~~	(coin)
4	5

flying

flame   coat

count   flying

coin   flash   flame   sly

float   floor   coin   join

join   sly

float   trying   frying

Name _____

1. How many cats were visiting Arnold? _____

2. Did Patty's mom and dad know how many cats were in the house? _____

3. Who had to stay behind while the other mice went out?

   _____

4. Was it day time or night time when the mice went out?

   _____

5. The mice were going to the _____ .

   • bedroom   • barn   • kitchen

6. How many cats were behind the mice? _____

7. Who was behind those cats? _____

8. How many cats were in front of the family? _____

Lesson 14   **31**

Three cats played tag.

1. What game did they play? _____

2. Draw a line through the word that tells the game they played.

3. Who played tag? _____

4. Circle the words that tell who played.

5. Write a **v** below the word **played.**

1. Make an **m** on the animal that squeaks.

2. Cross out the thing that comes from a bird.

shout •   • the king's wife

lazy •   • heating food

baboon •   • yell

queen •   • a kind of animal

kids •   • doesn't want to work

cooking •   • boys and girls

Name _____

1. How many cats were behind the mice? _____

2. How many cats were in front of the mice? _____

3. One cat started to leap on Patty's _____ .

   • mom   • sister   • brother

4. What did Patty shout? _____

5. What did the cat hit? _____

   • the ceiling   • the wall   • Bob

6. How long did the mice wait before they had a party?

   _____

7. They didn't have a party sooner because   • couldn't see
                                                      • were sleeping
   they _____ .   • couldn't hear

8. Did Patty have tears of joy or sadness?

   _____

Her old car shook loudly.

1. What shook loudly? _____

2. Circle the three words that tell what shook loudly.

3. What did the car do? _____

4. Make a line over the two words that tell what the car did.

5. Underline the word that has the letters **oo.**

whisper •   • brothers, sisters, mother, and father

field •   • jump on something

pounce •   • not a shout

bug •   • not hard

soft •   • an animal with six legs

family •   • a large place where grass grows

Name _____

1. The bragging rats were named

   _____ .

   • Gorman and Joan   • Bob and Pam   • Sherlock and Moe

2. What did the rats see on the ground? _____

   • a cat   • an ad   • a boy

3. The ad was for _____ .

   • new cars   • Bob   • a circus

4. Who told lies about doing circus tricks?

   _____

5. Who had a plan to make them be quiet?

   _____

   • Bob   • Sherlock and Moe   • the wise old rat

6. The wise old rat said that the rats would have a

   _____ .

   • boat   • circus   • race

7. Circle the things the rats would do at the circus.

- ride unicycles
- write a note
- juggle
- cut hair
- do trapeze tricks
- milk cows
- walk a tight rope

Three girls like eating ice cream.

---

1. What do they like eating? _____

2. Box the words that tell what they like eating.

3. How many girls like eating ice cream? _____

4. Make a star below the word that tells how many girls like eating ice cream.

---

lion •   • listened

window •   • things you read

clouds •   • It's made of glass.

heard •   • an animal that roars

night •   • They are seen in the sky.

books •   • a time when it's dark outside

Tubby the Tugboat

The fastest motorboats in the bay stayed at Dock Three. But one boat was slow. She was a smoky old tug named Tubby. Tubby was ten times slower than the other boats, but ten times stronger. Tubby's job was to push and pull the biggest ships in and out of the bay.

When Tubby honked her horn and went to work, the other boats got mad. "Stop making all that noise," they would say.

At the end of the day, when Tubby had put the last ship in place, she would go back to Dock Three. Tubby tried to keep quiet, but the other boats would complain. "Get that noisy tug out of here."

One night, a very bad storm raced into the bay. Waves crashed against the ships and barges. One big barge was blown out of place. The other boats woke up and started tugging at their ropes to get free. Tubby was still sleeping. Soon the barge was very close to the dock. The barge made three loud horn blasts.

Those blasts woke Tubby. Tubby thought it was time to work.

"Wow," Tubby said when she saw how close the barge was. "I don't know if I can stop that barge before it smashes everything."

"Oh, please try. Please," the other boats cried.

Tubby went between the barge and the dock. Then she pushed against the barge as hard as she could. Tubby pushed and puffed. The barge started moving slower and slower. Then it stopped. Then it moved slowly back.

"Tubby saved us," the other boats shouted.

But Tubby still had a lot of work. Finally she put that barge in place.

Tubby's motor worked so hard that Tubby stopped. Her motor had blown up.

One of the boats that had been mean to Tubby got free and raced into the bay. He grabbed Tubby's tow rope and pulled her back. That boat had never worked so hard before, but he was glad to do it.

Today, Tubby's motor is fixed. Tubby still honks and puffs smoke and goes to work every morning. But the other boats don't complain. They are proud to have Tubby as their friend.

The end.

Mastery Test 2

Name _____

One day, Patty the mouse was outside of her house.
Sherlock and Moe were yelling in a field next to that house.
They were fighting about who was the best at diving.

Patty got tired of listening to them, so she shouted, "Be
quiet."

Did Sherlock and Moe stop bragging? Patty doesn't know.
Her shout sent the bragging rats flying to the other side of the
field.

---

1. pounce

2. gray

3. choice

4. joy

5. ch<u>ew</u>

1. sport

2. shadow

3. whisper

4. afraid

5. tickle

1. mind

2. through

3. circus

4. toward

5. book

Name _____

1. Where was the circus held? _____

  • in a tent   • in a house   • at Bob's place

2. Who was in charge of the circus?

  _____

  • Joan   • the wise old rat   • Gorman

3. What was the first contest? _____

  • riding unicycles   • juggling   • walking the tight rope

4. What was the next contest? _____

5. Could the bragging rats ride unicycles? _____

6. Could the bragging rats juggle? _____

7. What did the crowd do when the bragging rats tried to do

  their tricks? _____

  • cried   • slept   • laughed

The yellow dirt was gold.

1. What was the yellow dirt? _____

2. Make a box around the word that tells what the yellow dirt was.

3. Put a **V** below the word **was.**

4. Circle the word that tells what kind of dirt was gold.

1. Make a line over the thing that can bounce.

2. Circle the eye.

3. Cross out the thing that is a toy.

4. Box the thing you wear on your foot.

pool •   • a place to swim

burn •   • not slow

bright •   • set something on fire

shout •   • a room in your house for cooking

quick •   • yell

kitchen •   • very light and shiny

Name _____

1. Circle the first contest. Make a line under the last contest.

- riding unicycles
- riding tigers
- walking the tight rope
- doing tricks on a trapeze
- reading books
- juggling
- eating cakes

2. How many bragging rats fell off the trapeze?

_____

3. What did the crowd do? _____

- sing
- laugh
- clap

4. Which bragging rat won the juggling contest?

_____

- Moe
- Sherlock
- no one

5. What did the crowd think the rats were best at doing?

_____

- clowning
- juggling
- riding unicycles

6. Who said, "Here we go again"? _____

The cat was ready to pounce.

1. Make an **X** over the word **ready.**

2. Who was ready? _____

3. Circle the two words that tell who was ready.

4. What was the cat ready to do? _____

5. Box the word that tells what the cat was ready to do.

voice •   • went through the air

giggle •   • what you speak with

fence •   • a small laugh

flew •   • It goes around your yard.

explain •   • not loud

quiet •   • tell about something

| eyes | rats | people | shadow | mice |

Name _____

1. What was right between East Town and West Town?

   _____

   • a town   • a farm   • a pond

2. Who lived on the farm? _____

   • Bob   • a robber   • Goober

3. What did Goober play in the evening? _____

   • a violin   • games   • tag

4. Did the people in East Town and West Town like his music?

   _____

5. What didn't the people in these towns like?

   _____

   • Goober's violin   • Goober's pigs   • Goober's truck

6. If the wind was blowing to East Town, most people in that

   town would _____ .

   • go to his farm   • go inside   • go for a swim

7. What would some people have on their nose?

_____

- a clothespin   • a ring   • a shoe

| trapeze | violin | Goober | ladder | juggle | clowns |

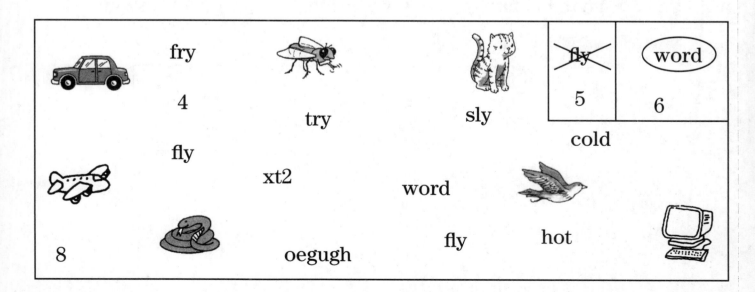

Name _____

 •

 •

 •

 •

 •

• "You bake dice busic."

• "I had my friends over for a pouncing party."

• "My voice is very, very loud."

• "Okay, baby."

• "Goober needs to give his pigs a bath."

• "Everybody laughs when I do my clown tricks."

1. Write the word **stamp** in the box.
2. Circle the letter that comes after **s.**
3. Make a box around the last letter.
4. Make a line over the letter that comes before **p.**
5. Cross out the **a.**

1. Wind blowing east made the smell from Goober's farm

   go to _____ .

   - East Town   • West Town   • North Town

2. When the wind was not blowing, who could stay outside?

   _____

   - nobody   • everybody   • only the little girl

3. Did a lot of people visit Goober? _____

4. One summer morning, who went to visit Goober?

   _____

   - two men   • his mother   • the little girl

5. What did she take with her?

   _____

   - her mother   • a coat   • a package

6. Where did she find Goober?

   _____

   - in the house   • in the barn   • in the yard

7. She said, "You bake dice busic." What was she trying to

   say? _____

Name _____

- "Everyone thinks my pigs really stink."

- "I'll take a package to him every week."

- "I broke my tooth on a turtle shell."

- "What happened to my lovely red sport car?"

- "There is one way to settle this argument."

1. Write the word **snooze** in the box.

2. Circle the letter that does not make a sound.

3. Box the letter before **n.**

4. Cross out the letter after **n.**

Lesson 21   **49**

1. Who visited Goober? _____

  • his mom   • his dad   • a little girl

2. She told Goober his pigs needed to take a _____ .

  • trip   • bath   • pill

3. What did she leave with Goober? _____

  • a package   • a pet   • a pig

4. What was inside? _____

  • bars of pig soap   • soap and clothes   • food and clothes

5. Did Goober give his pigs a bath? _____

6. How did he think they smelled when he was done?

   _____

  • good   • bad   • strange

7. Did the girl ever visit Goober again? _____

8. How do Goober's pigs smell now? _____

  • good   • bad   • strange

Name _____

feet •   • They are all over birds.

hands •   • They are at the end of legs.

feathers •   • They live on farms.

cows •   • They are what you read.

fences •   • They are at the end of arms.

books •   • They go around yards.

snowflake	song

_____ <u>snowball</u> _____

don't mud doors

~~doors~~	music
5	6

music doorway music must

  muddy music

doors

22

1. How did Honey get her name?

   _____

   • She was old.   • She was sweet.   • She was yellow.

2. Was Honey mean or nice? _____

3. What was the one thing she did not like? _____

   • mice   • cats   • mean dogs

4. One of her best pals was a _____ .

   • cat   • pig   • mouse

5. Andrea was very _____ .

   • shy   • big   • old

6. One day a woman came over with _____ .

   • a table   • a robot   • Sweetie

7. Who did Sweetie chase? _____

   • Andrea   • the woman   • Honey

8. Did that make Honey feel happy? _____

Name _____

- I gave my pigs a bath in a pond.

- I was trapped inside a table cloth.

- I love to make music.

- A little mouse gave me a big bite.

- Someone gave me a package.

| thief | camping | Tubby | unhappy |

foot _____   spider _____

_____   _____   _____

Lesson 23

1. Who did Sweetie chase? _____

2. What got stuck on Sweetie's claws?

   _____

- a table
- a table cloth
- a wash cloth

3. What were the only parts of Sweetie that stuck out?

   _____

- his nose and tail
- his paws
- his ears

4. What did Honey do to teach him a lesson?

   _____

- bit his nose
- barked at him
- bit his tail

5. Where did Honey go after teaching Sweetie a lesson?

   _____

- in the kitchen
- in the hall
- outside

6. Who did Sweetie think bit him?

   _____

- Honey
- Andrea
- Sweetie

7. Does Sweetie chase mice now? _____

8. Does Sweetie chase birds now? _____

Name _____

1. Dot was Dud's _____ .

       • sister   • brother   • mom

2. Were Dot and Dud big dogs or small dogs?

_____

3. Dot and Dud worked at

_____ .

     • the pet store
     • the ranger station
     • the sea

4. How many other dogs were at the ranger station?

_____

5. Their job was to find lost

_____ .

     • mountain climbers
     • swimmers
     • goats

6. Who was the best work dog? _____

7. Who would get lost when he went out to find mountain

climbers? _____

      Lesson 24   **55**

yawn •   • something sweet and sticky

honey •   • something you do before napping

east •   • to wash something by rubbing hard

scrub •   • the other way from north

south •   • not in danger

safe •   • the other way from west

The big dog walked home.

1. Who walked home? _____

2. Box the words that tell who walked home.

3. Where did the dog walk? _____

4. Make a line under the word that tells where the big dog walked.

5. How did the big dog get home? _____

6. Write a **v** over the word that tells how the big dog got home.

Name _____

- "I like little birds and little mice."

- "Stop picking on my brother."

- "Don't you think my pigs have a strange smell?"

- "I will try hard. I will. I will."

- "Those red cars are a mess."

- "Not many people come to visit my farm."

- "I met somebody at the corner of First and Elm."

_____

1. Write the word **chair** on the line.

2. Box the two letters that make the first sound.

3. Make a line over the letter that makes the last sound.

4. Make a line under the two letters that make the second sound.

5. Draw what the word tells about.

draw here

1. Did the other dogs believe that Dud would work
   hard? _____

2. When the alarm sounded, it told the dogs that
   _____ was in danger.

   - Dud
   - a climber
   - a ranger

3. The dogs headed _____ .

   - north   - south   - west

4. At first, did Dud try to work hard? _____

5. What did he find that was more interesting than sniffing
   snow? _____

   - the climber   - a rabbit   - his shadow

6. He stopped playing with his shadow because the shadow
   _____ .

   - chased him   - went away   - turned around

7. Could Dud tell which way was north? _____

8. Which way did he end up going?

   _____

Patty the Mouse

There once was a very large mouse named Patty. She lived with her mom and dad and six brothers and nine sisters. All the other mice in her family spoke in a tiny voice. Patty could not speak in a tiny voice. She had a very loud voice.

The mice had to be quiet when they went out. A large gray cat named Arnold lived in the house. If Arnold found the mice while they were sneaking around looking for food, he would pounce on them. One night, Patty's mom and dad told her she could not go out with them because of her loud voice.

Patty's mom and dad were afraid because there were new smells in the house. Arnold had four cats visiting him. They were planning a pouncing party.

From the mouse hole, Patty watched her dad leading the way toward the kitchen. Suddenly, Patty saw three cats following her family into the kitchen.

Patty said to herself, "I must do something to save my family." Patty snuck through the mouse hole, along the edge of the rug, and down the hall. She was now behind the three cats, and the three cats were behind Patty's family.

Patty was going to tell her family, "Cats are behind you. Run." But then she saw two more cats in front of her family. If the mice started to run, they would run right into the cats who were waiting.

One of the cats behind the mice was getting very close to one of Patty's sisters. Patty shouted in her loudest voice, "WATCH OUT."

Patty's voice sent the cats flying. When those cats landed, they were howling and running as fast as they could go.

Three days later, Patty's family gave her a cheese party. Her dad said, "We are very proud of you. You are a brave mouse, and you saved us from those cats. Thank you." After that day Patty went out with her family whenever she wanted.

The end.

Mastery Test 3

Name _____

Poor little Andrea was being chased by a mean yellow cat named Sweetie. They had run down the hall and back into the room where Honey was standing. Honey was ready to help Andrea out, but before she could do anything, Andrea and Sweetie darted under the table. Sweetie tried to pounce on Andrea, but his claws got stuck on the table cloth. The table cloth came down over Sweetie like a big white net.

1. great
2. climbed
3. wrong
4. lodge
5. flew

1. people
2. argue
3. noisy
4. shadow
5. understand

1. danger
2. middle
3. tight
4. shoe
5. perform

Name _____

bed •   • It lives in water.

fish •   • You drink water from it.

glass •   • People live in it.

broom •   • It's a tool for sweeping.

house •   • It's a place for sleeping.

| hard | baby | stink | Dot |

 Okay, _____ .

 Do my pigs really _____ ?

 My sister is named _____ .

 That mouse can really bite

_____ .

1. Dud went past the ranger station and came to the

   _____ .

   • north mountains   • south lake   • ski lodge

2. He sniffed to find a _____ .

   • kitchen   • fire   • ranger

3. Who let him inside? _____

   • a man   • a woman   • a ranger

4. She gave him soup and _____ .

   • bones   • meat scraps   • corn

5. What did Dud do after he ate? _____

   • took a nap   • looked for Dot   • barked

6. Which dog found the lost climber? _____

7. Did the other dogs keep up with Dot? _____

8. Was the climber in good shape? _____

Name _____

1. When Dud was sleeping at the lodge, where were the

   other dogs? _____

   • on the mountain   • at the lodge   • at the station

2. Who came to pick Dud up? _____

3. Had the ranger found the lost climber? _____

4. When did the ranger plan to go out again?

   _____

   • that night   • early in the morning   • after noon

5. Did the other dogs complain about Dud getting lost?

   _____

6. When Dud first got into the truck, did he know Dot was

   lost? _____

7. Who stuck up for Dud when he was a puppy? _____

| argument | honk | noise | mice | genie |

I am not a very old

_____ .

There is one way to settle this

_____ .

I love little birds and

_____ .

When I talk, I make a lot of

_____ .

When I go to work, I say honk, honk,

_____ .

1. Write the letter **a** in the middle of the line.

2. Write the letter **e** before the letter **a.**

3. Write the letter **r** before the letter **e.**

4. Write the letter **d** after the letter **a.**

5. What word did you write? _____

_____

Name _____

1. Dud made up his mind to find _____.

    • the ski lodge   • the ranger station   • Dot

2. When the ranger opened the truck door, what did Dud do?

    _____

    • barked   • took a nap   • jumped out

3. Which way did he run? _____

4. Did the other dogs follow him? _____

5. At first, Dud would stop to _____.

    • jump and play   • snort and sniff   • bark and howl

6. Then he put his nose in the snow like a snow _____.

    • ball   • plow   • man

7. At last there was a slight smell of _____.

    • ham   • eggs   • Dot

_____   _____

1. Make an **h** on the first line.

2. Make an **n** on the next line.

3. Write an **i** between the **h** and **n.**

4. Write a **k** after the **n.**

5. Make a **t** before the **h.**

6. What word did you make? _____

---

crawl •   • a place where dogs stay

kennel •   • to move through the air

rabbit •   • move on your hands and knees

cloth •   • a place in the mountains where
                             people stay

lodge •   • an animal with long ears

fly •   • what clothes are made of

---

tub	shark	scrub	bark

         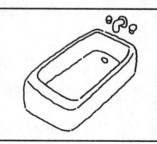

_____   _____   _____   _____

Name _____

| music | shadow | leaper | doctor | tooth |

_____

_____

_____

_____

window

_____

broom •

• You do it when you sleep.

dreaming •

math •

• You do it in school.

ladder •

snoring •

read •

• You do work with it.

Lesson 29   **69**

1. When Dud was closer to Dot, what happened to
   her smell? _____

   • It got stronger.   • It wasn't there.   • It got colder.

2. Did Dot think the climber could make it through the night?

   _____

3. The ranger put the climber on a little _____ .

   • cart   • sled   • log

4. Where did the ranger take the climber?

   _____

   • to the ski lodge   • to the mountains   • to the doctor

5. Did the other dogs think Dud was going to be good at his
   job? _____

6. What did the ranger give the dogs to thank them?

   _____

   • a card   • meat scraps and a bone   • soup

7. Who got the ham bone? _____

Name _____

1. What was Bill's last name? _____

2. What was his wife's first name? _____

3. Did Bill do a lot of nice things? _____

4. Did Bill have a problem? _____

5. What was his nickname? _____

   • Bob   • Boring Bull   • Boring Bill

6. When Bill started speaking, what did people do?

   _____

   • slip   • snore   • slurp

7. When Bill asked his wife what he should do, she said

   " _____ ."

   • Talk louder   • Sleep more   • Zzzz

8. Bill wanted to be less _____ .

Lesson 30

1. Box the king's wife.

2. Draw a cloud over the house.

3. Put an **X** on the roof of the bus.

4. Draw glasses on the queen's face.

window •   • mean

bridge •   • It's made of glass.

mud •   • not old

new •   • It goes over a stream.

giggle •   • wet dirt

nasty •   • a small laugh

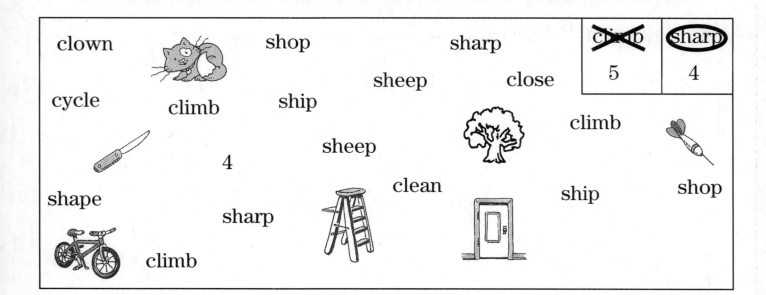

Name _____

1. Before the sleep expert came over, Bill was practicing in front of _____ .

   • his friends   • the mirror   • Milly

2. Bill tried to talk _____ .

   • faster and louder   • faster and slower   • louder and slower

3. What else did Bill try to do when he talked? _____

   • smell
   • smear
   • smile

4. The sleep expert was from

   _____ .

   • the Sleep More Clinic   • the farm   • Bob's place

5. Who put the expert to sleep? _____

6. When did the sleep expert want to come back? _____

   • tonight
   • never
   • tomorrow

7. Who did the expert want to bring with her? _____

   • patients
   • other experts
   • parents

The duck waddled near the pond.

1. What was the duck near? _____

2. Make a line under the two words that tell what the duck was near.

3. Make a **x** below the word **waddled.**

4. Draw a line through the two words that tell who waddled.

---

little •   • a place where grass grows

tiger •   • the day after yesterday

field •   • tiny

today •   • a large cat with stripes

stump •   • a cat's foot

paw •   • what's left after a tree is cut down

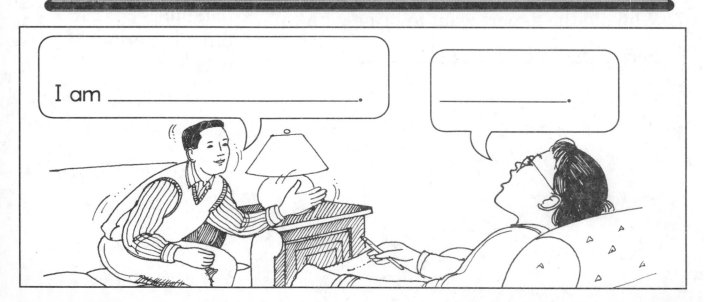

I am _____.

_____.

Name _____

1. How many experts from the Sleep More Clinic visited Bill?

   _____

2. Were all the experts happy about visiting Bill? _____

3. How many experts thought the visit was a waste of time?

   _____

4. The leader told the others to

   _____ .

   • ask good questions   • stay awake   • stop eating

5. After Bill talked to the experts for a while, they said,

   " _____ "

   • That was interesting.   • Thank you, Bill.   • Zzzz.

6. Who was the first expert to wake up?

   _____

7. How many experts were still sleeping when the others were

   ready to leave? _____

The man behind the horse was old.

1. Underline the two words that tell who was behind the horse.

2. Make an **A** over the last word.

3. Where was the man? _____

4. Box the three words that tell where the man was.

_____

ceiling •   • a large cat with a mane

hear •   • spend cash to get something

lion •   • listen to something

buy •   • the top of a room

lawn •   • not old

happy •   • glad

young •   • a grassy yard

_____

| puddle | peppers | patient | popcorn | ponies | party |

 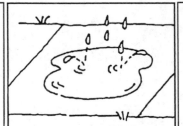  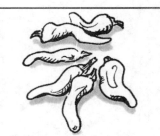

_____ _____ _____ _____

Name _____

1. How did Bill feel after the experts left his place?

   _____

2. Where was Bill at nine-thirty the next morning?

   _____

3. Was Bill able to put the first two patients to sleep?

   _____

4. Then Bill put _____ patients to sleep.

   - five   - twenty   - two

5. How many doctors fell asleep? _____

6. Who was the only one in the room left awake?

   _____

7. Do you think Bill will take the job at the clinic?

   _____

1. Box the thing that shows minutes and seconds.

2. Draw a hat on the guy.

3. Circle the young person.

4. Make a line under the person who had been a boy.

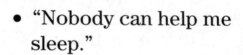

- "Nobody can help me sleep."

- "I'm just a boring kind of guy."

- "Snort. Zzzz."

- "Would you like to work at our clinic?"

- "Let me tell you something interesting."

Name _____

1. When Bill talked to people in his regular voice, they

   _____ .

2. Did Bill ever find a voice that did not put people to

   sleep? _____

3. Circle the ways that voice was different from his normal voice.

   - lower   - slower   - higher

   - louder   - faster   - softer

4. Does Bill use his high voice when he works with patients?

   _____

5. Do people still call him Boring Bill? _____

6. They call him _____ .

Bill asked good questions.

1. Box the two words that tell what he asked.

2. Circle the word that comes after the word **Bill.**

3. Who asked good questions? _____

4. Make a line through the word that tells who asked.

heard •	• a large cat with a mane
lion •	• a mother or father
parent •	• listened to
boil •	• a place for patients
clinic •	• not boring
interesting •	• make water really hot

Name _____

POPULAR TEXTBOOK STORIES

Number of Students: _____

Who do students want to read about?

	1	2	3	4	5	6	7	8	9	10	11	12
The Bragging Rats												
Tubby the Tug												
Rolla												
Molly and Bleep												
Patty and the Cats												
Goober												
Honey and Sweetie												
Dot and Dud												
Boring Bill												

1. _____

2. _____

3. _____

- "I'm just a boring kind of guy."

- "I found my sister."

- "I found the climber first."

- "Zzzz."

- "I didn't know north from south."

- "Some people like me to talk in my regular voice."

- "I don't let anyone pick on my brother."

His sister is a dog.

1. What is his sister? _____

2. Circle the word that tells what his sister is.

3. Box the word that comes before **is.**

4. Make a line over the word that starts with the letter **i.**

5. Cross out both words that have three letters.

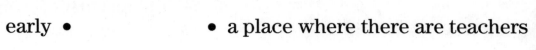

early •   • a place where there are teachers

popular •   • not late

school •   • when lots of people like you

clinic •   • It has water all around it.

boring •   • not interesting

island •   • a place where there are doctors

| mirror | disappear | magic | lady |

_____   mountain   _____

school _____   _____   _____

The Circus

One spring day, the bragging rats saw an ad on the ground for a circus. At once they started to brag.

Sherlock said he was the best at doing circus tricks. Moe said he could do better tricks than Sherlock could ever dream of doing. The rats shouted for a long time. The wise old rat said, "There is only one way to settle this.

We will have a circus. We will see which one of you does the best circus tricks."

So all of the rats worked very hard to set up a circus tent. On the day of the circus, they gathered in the tent.

The first contest was juggling nuts. The bragging rats threw their nuts in the air. Most of them landed on the ground. One landed on Sherlock's head. The crowd roared with laughter.

The wise old rat said, "For the next contest, the rats will ride unicycles."

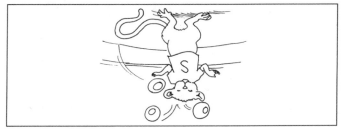

Both bragging rats tried to ride at the same time. They got on. They ran into each other. They fell down. And they did a lot of yelling at each other. "You knocked me down. Stay out of my way."

The crowd laughed a lot.

After the bragging rats tried to juggle and ride unicycles, they tried walking the tight rope. Both of the rats quickly fell off the tight rope. Then crowd laughed. The last contest was the trapeze.

Both the rats tried to get on the same trapeze, but soon both of them were hanging by one paw. Then they were hanging by no paws. Ouch.

The rats in the crowd laughed so loudly that they could not hear the bragging rats yelling at each other. After the laughter stopped, everybody voted for the rat that did the best circus tricks.

The rat pack didn't think either bragging rat was good at circus tricks. But all of them agreed that the bragging rats were the best clowns anybody had ever seen.

The end.

fold first

Take-Home 4

fold

Mastery Test 4

Name _____

   Bill tried to say things that would interest other people. He asked questions and tried to get people to talk about themselves. He tried to say things that were funny. He tried to talk faster and louder. He tried to smile more when he talked. But all those changes made no difference. After Bill was through speaking, everybody else was sleeping. That is why people called him "Boring Bill." That made Bill very sad.

1. station	1. doctor	1. patient
2. remember	2. tomorrow	2. answer
3. lady	3. swerve	3. amazing
4. practice	4. except	4. regular
5. certainly	5. change	5. expert